Who Are You?
See It, Say It, and Seize It

by DeWayne Hendrix

DORRANCE
PUBLISHING CO
EST. 1920
PITTSBURGH, PENNSYLVANIA 15238

Dorrance Publishing Co
585 Alpha Drive
Pittsburgh, PA 15238
Visit our website at *www.dorrancebookstore.com*

Interior Design by Tracy Reedy

ISBN: 978-1-4809-9162-0
eISBN: 978-1-4809-9376-1

Affirmation Creed

I am somebody. Although some have labeled me worthless, I know my value.

My current situation will not deter me from living out my purpose.

Too increase my total wellness, I will take advantage of all educational, recreational, and spiritual learning opportunities available to me.

I take full responsibility for my past, present, and future actions.

When I get frustrated, I will seek clarity.

When I am rejected, I will keep a cool head.

When I am depressed, I will stop feeling sorry for myself and get a grip.

When faced with temptation to live my old life, I will exercise my will power.

I will not give up.

I will continue to press forward.

I will act in accordance with my rights, duties, and privileges as a citizen and be a contributing member to my community.

I will make a difference.

Strengthening Critical Thinking Skills

Critical Thinking

The foundation of this book is to understand principles of critical thinking. Imperial research suggests that people begin developing critical thinking competencies at a very young age. Paul (1992) defines critical thinking as the disciplined mental activity of evaluating arguments and propositions and making judgments that can guide the development of beliefs and taking action. Critical thinking can also be defined as good, rational, effective, and persuasive thinking.

A portrait of an ideal critical thinker is someone who is inquisitive in nature, open-minded, flexible, and fair-minded, has a desire to be well informed, understands diverse viewpoints, and is willing to both suspend judgment and to consider other perspectives (Facione, 1990). Critical thinkers can summarize complex arguments and evidence, understand opposing positions, draw reasonable conclusions, predict logical sequences, devise sensible alternatives, and solve complex problems.

Critical thinking is the intellectually disciplined process of actively and skillfully conceptualizing, applying, analyzing, synthesizing, and/or evaluating information gathered from, or generated by, observation, experience, reflection, reasoning, or communication as a guide to belief and action. In its exemplary form, it is based on universal intellectual values that transcend subject matter divisions: clarity, accuracy, precision, consistency, relevance, sound evidence, good reasons, depth, breadth, and fairness.

Instructions aimed at improving student's critical thinking skills have generally shown positive results (Kennedy, 1991). This book will take the readers on a journey through their past and assist them with using critical thinking methods to evaluate and access some of the core concepts and subjects of this program, which includes:

- Accessing personal strengths and areas for improvement.
- Evaluating past and present interpersonal relationships.
- Understanding the power of forgiveness.
- Importance of Total Wellness.
- Developing a Personal Strategic Plan.
- Making a Difference.

While reading this book, you will be sensitized to deep rooted problem structure and asked to elevate their focus to deeper levels below the surface and general aspects of issues and tasks (Willingham, 2007). It is important you begin to "think about thinking" as each chapter will allow you to forge on a path to evaluate the foundations of decision making and what factors lead into making choices and taking action.

....

Case Study: Decisions, Decisions

Lee is a high school senior who works at a local shoe store, and he just received notification that he has been accepted to two colleges in Texas near where both of his parents are from and his extended family lives. Lee only applied to both of those schools because he was excited about leaving in the Los Angeles area and attend college in a more rural setting as he always enjoyed going to the south for summer vacations. Lee chose the two specific schools near his family because his cousins, Corey and Jayleen, graduated from those schools. Lee is the last of his parent's four children, and none of his older siblings attended college. Lee's father is a high school graduate and an armed forces veteran and is now an oil refinery operator. Lee's mother did not graduate from high school as she became pregnant with his oldest sister during her senior year and dropped out of school, and she is currently a housewife.

Lee had not discussed his plans for after college with his parents, and when he received his letters of acceptance, he wanted to talk with them, so he could decide which college he should attend. To his surprise, when he met with his parents, they were not as excited as he was about getting accepted into college. Lee's mom asked him who was going to be paying for the tuition because they could not afford it, and when he looked to his dad for support, he just shrugged his shoulders. Lee's parents told him if they could afford it, they would help him and suggested he enroll in a junior college and save his money, and in a couple of years, he could maybe attend the school of his choice.

Lee, visibly frustrated, went to his room and became depressed. Over the next few weeks, he was trying to figure out what he should do because he desperately wanted to leave the urban environment he grew up in and get away from all of the violence in his community.

....

You Make the Call

Lee has several strategies he can choose from to eventually achieve his goal of attending college in Texas. If you were hired to advise Lee which of the below choices would you recommend.

A. Go to a Junior College and save money to attend the college of his choice in Texas after earning an Associate's Degree.

B. Save money and sit out his first semester and attend the college of his choice in the spring semester.

C. Give up on his dream of college and find a job to support himself.

D. Choose a different option for Lee.

....

Self-Assessment

1. How would you best describe the way you make decisions?
   - ❏ Impulsive
   - ❏ Indecisive
   - ❏ Analyze, Weigh Options, Decide

2. How often do you include others and weigh their opinions when making decisions?

Affirmation Creed

I am somebody. Although some have labeled me worthless, I know my value.

My current situation will not deter me from living out my purpose.

Too increase my total wellness, I will take advantage of all educational, recreational, and spiritual learning opportunities available to me.

I take full responsibility for my past, present, and future actions.

When I get frustrated, I will seek clarity.

When I am rejected, I will keep a cool head.

When I am depressed, I will stop feeling sorry for myself and get a grip.

When faced with temptation to live my old life, I will exercise my will power.

I will not give up.

I will continue to press forward.

I will act in accordance with my rights, duties, and privileges as a citizen and be a contributing member to my community.

I will make a difference.

Knowing Your Worth and Accessing Your Personal Strengths and Areas for Improvement

The affirmation creed begins with, "I am somebody, although some have labeled me worthless, I know my value." Meaning has been characterized as the degree to which people feel their lives are significant, as well as the attachment to something bigger than themselves (Steger, Frazier, Oishi & Kaler, 2006).

Maslow's hierarchy of needs (1943) is a model that has been taught for many years in various subjects and used in many curriculums to understand human behavior and individual motivating factors. Maslow wanted to understand what motivates people. He believed that people possess a set of motivation systems unrelated to rewards and inconspicuous desires. Maslow (1943) stated people are motivated to achieve certain needs. These five motivational needs are physiological, safety, love/belonging, esteem, and self-actualization. Later, these are expanded to Transcendence needs (Maslow, 1970). They were expanded to cognitive needs, aesthetic needs, and transcendence needs.

To create a plan or vision for your life, you must set objectives and visualize your goals and then develop strategies to create a path to attain them. People who are blind cannot see naturally through their eyes, and for them to move about without assistance from others at all times, they use their internal vision and other important basic human instincts, such as their sense of touch, smell, and sounds to accomplish their tasks. Those skills had to be developed through strategy. I used this analogy because persons who can see through our natural eyes must also utilize their insightful instincts to achieve the results they want to accomplish in life. Many times people impose self-doubt principles to their worth because they feel as if they do not possess the skills to accomplish a certain goal or task, or it may be directly linked to what others have told them about what their worth is.

Self-doubt is defined as the experience of general uncertainty about one's competence coupled with an intense preoccupation over prospective failure and negative evaluation (Jones & Berglas, 1978). Self-doubt stems from the absence of a strong desired self-prospective success that can sustain ongoing feelings of self-confidence and competence by effectively organizing energy and goal-directed action (Carroll, Arkin & Shade, 2011). If you are in a place or space of self-doubt and you do not think you are worthy, please know that you are more and you have value.

In a world that is based on the economy, trade, goods, services, and brand labeling, often we place our own self-worth on what others think of us. If you are incarcerated in the natural sense, or in your mind due to a personal issue or addiction, negative labels are often attached and stuck to you. It is also not unusual for family members or close friends to associate you with an infirmity when discussing you when you are not present.

These family members, friends, or associates may introduce you in gossip-like conversation in manners such as, "that is my cousin that just got out of jail," or "that's my sister who got pregnant when she was 15, and my momma still raising her kid," or "that is my brother who think he is better than the rest of us because after he graduated from college and got a big-time paying job and got a big house with a pool, and the rest of us are still living at home or in an apartment," and finally, "that is my favorite aunt because she always has my back, no matter what I do."

Whether it's a positive label or negative label, in someone else's eyes, we have been labeled in one way or another. One of the key components to discuss in this book is that although you may be in a tough situation, your life does not have to be defined by your current situation or social and/or economic status. You are somebody, it doesn't matter what others think of you, and how you see yourself is going to determine your future success or failure. How you conduct yourself and what kind of vision you have for your life will be the key factors in developing your vision to get past whatever is hindering you.

It is important to acknowledge your personal strengths and areas for improvement. Knowing the strengths you possess will make you stronger and will help you continue to build your character when you use your strengths for the right reasons. You also should have a posture to seek to further pursue educational, recreational, and spiritual opportunities to continue to develop your character strengths.

You should never be ashamed to admit your areas for improvement. Developing meaningful relationships with people who have character strengths you do not possess, along with working diligently to improve on them, may have a significant impact on your future achievements. This type of thought process will give you momentum and a positive vibe as you pursue different outcomes that may be currently plaguing you. As you continue to build upon your strengths and areas for improvement, your self-worth will increase.

Case Study: Peer Pressure

A young man named M.C. was entering the 7th grade in Phoenix, Arizona and was looking forward to continuing to learn how to play the trumpet and being a member of the basketball team. M.C. was earning an allowance of $20 per week if he completed all of his chores. His parents just increased his allowance from $10 dollars because he was entering middle school. During the first week of school, some of his friends were making fun of him because he didn't have enough money to buy lunch at school and had to bring something from home. It was a cool thing in middle school to buy lunch from the cafeteria. M.C. felt bad that he was being teased and wondered how he could get more allowance from his parents. A few weeks after school started, M.C. began attending basketball practices for the upcoming season. One day before practice, a cousin of one of M.C.'s teammates named Joe Ray approached M.C. and asked him if he wanted to earn some extra money. Joe Ray was an older kid in the neighborhood who sold drugs, and M.C. had known him since he was younger. Joe Ray told M.C. if he would become a lookout for him, he could earn $40 for three hours of work per day he worked as a lookout. He also told M.C. that where he would be looking out for the police would be low risk location because where he would stand, he could conceal himself easily.

M.C. instantly thought about getting that extra money he needed to be a cool kid, like his friends, and told Joe Ray he would think about it and get back to him. After going home and pondering what Joe Ray had offered, M.C. began to think about one of his uncles who had been in and out of jail because of a drug addiction and the issues he has caused for everyone in their family. He recalled a time when his uncle, who lived with him and his family, owed a drug dealer $100 dollars and didn't pay him back and he called their house and threatened to kill everyone in the family, and his parents had to change their phone number. Plus, his parents were very restrictive of him, and it would be hard for him to be unaccounted for to be a lookout for a drug dealer, and besides, Joe Ray had just spent several months in juvenile camp prior to asking M.C. to be a lookout. After careful thought, M.C. respectfully told Joe Ray that he could not be a lookout for him and would live with the small allowance his parents were providing for him.

....

You Make the Call

Review the below questions and think about how M.C. was able to make the decision to not begin a life of crime and potentially compromise his future.

1. What were some of the consequences if M.C. had made a different choice?
2. What were some of the critical thinking strategies M.C. used to make his final decision?

....

Self-Assessment

1. How often do you assess your personal strengths and areas for improvement?
2. Do you attribute any of your strengths and areas for improvement to your personal and professional relationships?

Affirmation Creed

I am somebody. Although some have labeled me worthless, I know my value.

My current situation will not deter me from living out my purpose.

Too increase my total wellness, I will take advantage of all educational, recreational, and spiritual learning opportunities available to me.

I take full responsibility for my past, present, and future actions.

When I get frustrated, I will seek clarity.

When I am rejected, I will keep a cool head.

When I am depressed, I will stop feeling sorry for myself and get a grip.

When faced with temptation to live my old life, I will exercise my will power.

I will not give up.

I will continue to press forward.

I will act in accordance with my rights, duties, and privileges as a citizen and be a contributing member to my community.

I will make a difference.

Evaluating Positive and Negative Relationships from Your Past and Present

Humans are creatures of relationship and close relationships are a source for a meaningful life (Van Tongeren, Green, Nook, Davis & Ramos, 2015). Typically, our value system is created and developed by our parents, that teach us our social norms, and secondly, other family members, community leaders, such as our teachers, and religious leaders help facilitate how we view and treat interpersonal relationships. Empirical work has been validated regarding the importance of social connections in maintaining a sense of meaning in life. (Von Tongeren, Green, Nook, Davis & Ramos, 2015)

Depending on what we learn and how to navigate through our early relationships, it determines how we value ourselves and the people we are close to. In this book, I have placed a strong emphasis on acknowledging the positive and negative relationships each reader has had up to this juncture in life to illustrate the impact that these interactions had on your lives. How we define positive and negative relationships in this book is as follows: a positive relationship is an interaction with someone that is based on good ethics and integrity that has benefited your life, for example, someone who has been there for you but has also held you accountable when you may have done something wrong. As fundamentally social creatures (Baumeister & Leary, 1995), humans thrive in close relationships.

A negative relationship is defined as an interaction with someone who has impacted your life in such a diminishing way where they may have been doing things that has led your life down a path of destruction, persons that make you question your self-worth and value, and individuals that you made life altering decisions when you were with them.

Looking very closely at these relationships may change your view of positive and negative relationships. It may also change the way you view yourself. First, you must define for yourself what is your value system? What are your ethics? How do you define integrity? What are your morals? Have the answers to these questions changed since you have been in your current situation? These questions must be thoroughly reviewed and answered before determining who has been a positive and negative influence on your life. Additionally, you must more importantly ask yourself who you have had a positive and negative influence on.

Once you have the courage to ask these very important questions and answer them truthfully and honestly, you can begin to make decisions on who will remain in your life moving forward, who will be dismissed, and who you need to remove yourself from. Because you walked away from people from your past doesn't mean they are a bad person or that you are better than them, it just means that you were not good together and both of you will be better off without each other. At times, people need to admit some relationships bring the worst out in us.

Looking into your past can be hurtful and also bring a sense of joy when thinking of people who meant you well and made you feel loved and valued. Acknowledging your past and taking responsibility for what has went right and wrong in your lives will put you in a better position to have a brighter future as we forge ahead. Taking this inventory will also put us in a position to forgive yourself and others who may have harmed us.

....

Case Study: When to Let Go

Danette and Elle have been friends since they were infants, in fact, they have known each other so long, the first time they met, they were several months old. Their parents were close friends, and they lived two houses from each other on a quiet street. Throughout their childhood, they were inseparable; they played on the high school soccer team, sang in the church choir together, and stayed up most nights talking on the phone with each other. After they both enrolled in college together down state, it appeared that Elle and Danette were going to be life-long friends. However, after they both started their first semester, Elle and Danette began to grow a part. Elle, the more adventurous one of the two, began partying late at night and started smoking marijuana. Although both Danette and Elle drank beer and other alcoholic drinks in high school, Danette did not want to advance to the next level and start smoking marijuana.

Danette and Elle were roommates and lived in a suite with two other young ladies, and Elle became more attached to them because they liked to party as well. Elle and her other roommates started teasing Danette and calling her "square and uptight". Danette felt like an outcast and wanted to begin distancing herself from Elle, but she couldn't because she was "family." Danette began focusing on her school work and started a part-time work study job at a local supermarket. She helped Elle get a job as well, and she thought this was going to help their friendship. However, Elle started stealing from the supermarket with the help of their roommates. Eventually, Elle was fired and while Danette was questioned; she was not let go because she did not have anything to do with what Elle was responsible for.

Danette began to evaluate her life and her friendship with Elle. She had an opportunity to move into another dorm room but was nervous about doing so because she didn't know how it was going to affect her friendship with Elle, and she didn't want her parents to get involved with their situation. Danette is determined to stay focused on school, maintaining her employment, and having fun when she has the chance to.

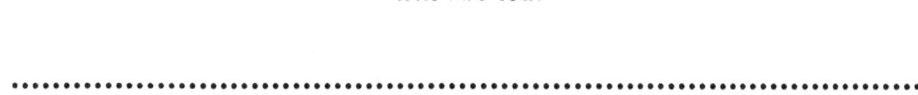

You Make the Call

At each stage of life, it is important to evaluate the relationships we have in our lives. If you were hired as a consultant to advise Danette which choice would you choose regarding her relationship with Elle.

A. Stay in the apartment with Elle and roommates and hope things get better.

B. Move into another dorm room and remain friends with Elle from a distance.

C. Move into another dorm room and completely distance herself from Elle.

D. Another option.

Self-Assessment

1. How often do you assess your positive and negative relationships? How have they shaped you into the person you are?

2. What factors are weighed when determining if a relationship is having a positive or negative impact on your life?

Affirmation Creed

I am somebody. Although some have labeled me worthless, I know my value.

My current situation will not deter me from living out my purpose.

Too increase my total wellness, I will take advantage of all educational, recreational, and spiritual learning opportunities available to me.

I take full responsibility for my past, present, and future actions.

When I get frustrated, I will seek clarity.

When I am rejected, I will keep a cool head.

When I am depressed, I will stop feeling sorry for myself and get a grip.

When faced with temptation to live my old life, I will exercise my will power.

I will not give up.

I will continue to press forward.

I will act in accordance with my rights, duties, and privileges as a citizen and be a contributing member to my community.

I will make a difference.

Understanding the Impact Your Current Situation has made on Your Family and Friends

Change the Conversation, Change the Culture

Support is a very important component to have when dealing with any life changing issues. Most notably, support comes from family and friends. To garner the kind of support you truly need, taking your current situation seriously will help create the type of communication needed to help see you through the process of moving forward. True support comes from people who will hold you accountable, yet will hold your hand, give you positive affirmation, remind you how important you are, and give you the space to make the appropriate decisions to turn your life around. As discussed earlier in the book, some topics are taboo in families and community circles, and it is easier to think something about someone or talk behind their back rather than speak to them directly to express your feelings.

Having discussions related not only about your issues are others can be difficult, especially if these types of conversations have not been a part of the past. If you change the type of conversations you have, you can change the culture around you. For far too long, generational curses have haunted families and communities because people accept things as the way they are and have been in the past. It it's now time for people to step up and stop the cycle of fear, failure, lack of faith to start something new and change a generation. While learning from your past will help you define who you want to become, people must leverage the things that they need to improve their life and make the necessary adjustments.

It is imperative that the plans you make to become a new and improved person, they must be included. It is healthy to discuss how much the person's criminal activities, drug abuse, and absenteeism has burdened the family and made those around you have to dig deeper to stand in the gap that you should be. Also, if you are telling your kids you are away at school when you really are in jail or an in-patient program, you need to ask yourself when is it appropriate to tell your children where you really are. At some point, you are going to need to tell them the truth because they are a part of you and you do not want them to take the same path you took and you do not want someone else telling your story for you.

Commit yourself to stop having small talk all the time and avoiding the inevitable. In too many families, the person who does not show up to the reunion or cookout is the one who gets talked about the most. Gossip will never be eliminated; however, it can be significantly reduced if we do more listening than talking. If we admit where we are and express where we want to be and not carry on gossip conversations, many broken relationships can be healed.

Beyond having conversations that will help bridge the gap to gain the support you need is to not be in a relationship where you are manipulating family and friends or being enabled. Your life will not change for the better if you are using persons to provide you things that are not legal or moral while you are in your current situation. If you are dealing with substance abuse issues, family and friends should not be providing you with these items. If you are incarcerated, people who visit you should not be bring you drugs or any other type of contraband. This only exacerbates your problems. You need people who are going to hold you accountable, not enablers or persons dealing with the same issues as you. People who do not respect the rule of law and have low moral standards have no place in your life.

· ·

Case Study: A Story of an Enablers Mindset

Sometime ago, a young lady named Lisa was going to visit her son's father named Jodie at the local jail. He was facing a ten year sentence for conspiracy to sell drugs. Lisa and Jodie were supposed to get married before he was arrested a few months ago. Although Jodie's arrest upset Lisa she planned to marry him because he had treated her better than any other of her past lovers. Lisa had been to the jail to visit Jodie a few times, and the last visit, he asked her the next time she came to the jail for her to bring him some drugs because he needed a hit. Lisa did not approve of Jodie's lifestyle, but because he was a good supporter of her and her family, she dealt with it. Lisa was reluctant to bring in drugs but felt guilty if she didn't because of all the things that Jodie had done for her in the past.

Lisa contacted one of Jodie's associates named Bricks, got the drugs, and decided on visiting day she would smuggle the drugs into the jail. Since she had not done this before, she was nervous and had to ask Bricks how she could get the drugs in without being detected. Lisa talked with Jodie and tried to speak in code but made a mistake and said I spoke with Bricks and I got the stuff to get to you. Staff at the jail randomly monitored phone calls and was alerted that Lisa may try and contraband to Jodie. On the day of the visit, Jodie made it through the screening site and got into the visiting room. What she and Jodie didn't know was that staff in the investigative office were monitoring the visiting room and was waiting for her to attempt to give Jodie some drugs. After a few minutes, Lisa went to buy something from the vending machine and bought two of the same items. Both Lisa and Jodie opened their item at the same time and Lisa gave him the drugs, and at that point, the investigative staff stormed into the visiting room, placed handcuffs on Jodie, and escorted Lisa from the visiting room.

As Lisa waited to find out if she was going to be arrested, she immediately began thinking of her son and what is going to happen to him if both parents were in jail. She began having visions of Child Protective Services, visiting her mother's apartment and taking him away. The jail administrator came into the area where they were holding Lisa and let her know that she would not be allowed to visit the facility in the future. He went on to tell her that she should be arrested for introducing drugs into a correctional institution, but the local police department was contacted, but due to legality concerns regarding jurisdiction, they would not be dispatched to the jail. He asked Lisa if she had any children and she said yes and began to cry. He finally told her that this is a sign for her to get her life together because both of her son's parents could have been in jail today, and if she does not make some changes very soon, her son could grow up without both parents.

. . . .

You Make the Call

Far to often people feel obligated to carry out favors for others in return for what people have done for them in the past. Bricks request of Lisa has her on the brink of making some decisions that may alter her and her children's future forever. If you were Lisa's spiritual conscious how would you advise her to critically think her way out of this dilemma.

1. What do you think Lisa should do from here?
2. What factors do you believe led Lisa to bringing the drugs into the facility?
3. How can Lisa withdraw from an enablers mind set?

. . . .

Self-Assessment

1. What factors are attributed to topics being taboo and not discussed in families and other close relationships?
2. What strategies can be applied to develop the ability to begin having difficult discussions?

Affirmation Creed

I am somebody. Although some have labeled me worthless, I know my value.

My current situation will not deter me from living out my purpose.

Too increase my total wellness, I will take advantage of all educational, recreational, and spiritual learning opportunities available to me.

I take full responsibility for my past, present, and future actions.

When I get frustrated, I will seek clarity.

When I am rejected, I will keep a cool head.

When I am depressed, I will stop feeling sorry for myself and get a grip.

When faced with temptation to live my old life, I will exercise my will power.

I will not give up.

I will continue to press forward.

I will act in accordance with my rights, duties, and privileges as a citizen and be a contributing member to my community.

I will make a difference.

The Power of Forgiveness

Research has concluded that close relationships are a source of joy and meaning, and they can also be a source of betrayal and pain. After an interpersonal relationship has been torn, forgiveness can serve as a function of restoration to some of the meaning that may have been lost (Van Tengren, Welch, Davis, Green & Worthington, 2012).

The power of forgiveness is so strong that it can uproot deep stressors that may have plagued us for many years, and broken relationships are at the heart of this subject. Harvard Researcher and Physician George Vaillant describes forgiveness as one of the eight positive emotions that keep us connected with our deepest selves and others. He considers these positive emotions to be the key ingredient that binds us together in our humanity and they include love, hope, joy, compassion, faith, awe, and gratitude.

While going through and inventorying relationships are critical to putting you in position to have better interpersonal interactions, the most important relationship are the one you have with yourself. Forgiveness transforms anger and hurt into healing and peace, and before you can forgive others who may have forsaken you, you must forgive yourself first for the transgressions you committed against yourself and others. Having the ability to acknowledge your wrongs and taken account for what you've done first will add to your character strengths. Dr. Randy Kamen describes a strategy model to learning forgiveness in an article in the Huffington Post in 2009; 1. Inquire deeply about the root of your anger or grudge; 2. Review your grievance story and reengineer the story, so you use yourself in a more empowered way; 3. Develop capacity for empathy and compassion for yourself and landing in a painful situation; 4. Create new associations with your old story of neglect and abuse.

For some people, the things they do not want to let go may have been things that has haunted them and their family for years. Whether it is socially or economically based, people tend to hold onto things in their families and blame everyone for where they are now. Generational curses are real and being adversely impacted by being raised by a single parent or having family members in the 3rd or 4th consecutive generation of incarceration due to criminal activity or behavior altering addictions, such as drug and alcohol abuse, is a reason to raise concerns but is not ultimately an excuse not to forgive. If you are aware enough to acknowledge these issues that may be burdening you, you have the will and the power to forgive and develop strategies to break those strongholds and generational curses. Not only will the power of forgiveness change the course of your life but also the generations that follow you. It takes courage to overcome fear and be the first to say "I forgive you," it doesn't mean the circumstance wins and you become a doormat, but what it means is you will ultimately win.

Fred Luskin talks about the way we develop our grievance story in his book *Forgive for Good*. Your story is the one you tell over and over and over to yourself, and possibly others, about the way you were maltreated and the way you became victimized. Luskin teaches us to cast our story in such a way that we become a survivor of difficult times and be the hero of our story.

Developing empathy for others may alter many of our relationships. Letting go may also have a significant impact on your health. Stressors may be reduced, your blood pressure may be reduced, and you may have a better outlook on various other aspects of your life, maybe a result of just releasing the burdens we often carry. You can control your thoughts and actions, however you cannot control the behavior of others. Moving on and letting from your past mistakes is a sign of growth and maturity.

....

Case Study: A Story about the Power of Forgiveness

A young man named Travis had just finished college and was ready to forge out on his own after landing a job in the year 2000 in a city on the opposite coast he was raised in. As he began to plan his upcoming move, he started to think about how much he was going to miss his family and friends, but moreover, his sense of disappointment that neither of his brothers would be in a position to help him prepare to start his new chapter in life. His thoughts of disappointment came from never developing the type of little-big brother relationships with them because of the circumstances that lead to their lack of close relations. The only memories of his eldest brother Kane were a Tonka truck he bought him when he was four years-old, just before Kane moved to Alabama when he turned 19 to live with his grandparents. The next time Travis saw Kane was when the family visited Alabama on a vacation in 1980. By then, Kane was married with one son and eventually had four more sons and named two of his boys after Travis. Travis would not see Kane for another 22 years and had very few phone conversations, this was due to Kane leaving his family and moving to Chicago to pursue unknown goals and becoming an alcoholic and drug abuser. In 1988, Kane committed a violent crime, which led him to receiving a 20-year sentence. Travis often thought what it would have been like to have a close relationship with Kane, especially since he named two of his sons after him. Due to Kane's actions, Travis did not develop a close relationship with his nephews.

Travis had a relationship with his second eldest brother, Clyde, but it wasn't as close as Clyde thought it was. Clyde was seven years older than Travis, and they shared a room together. Clyde would take Travis to the mall on the weekends and do other things for him, but Travis had a secret disdain for Clyde because he was a homosexual. Travis would often get teased by his schoolmates as early as the 2nd grade. Boys would say nasty things about Clyde and as Travis got older, when people would ask if he was his brother, Travis would deny him. Because of Travis's religious beliefs, being gay or a homosexual was not accepted and his family never openly discussed the topic, even though everyone knew Clyde's status. In 1994, Clyde became visibly sick, and informed his family he had the AIDS disease. This was a turning point on how the family would view Clyde's homosexuality and the relationship Travis had with Clyde. Clyde nearly died in 1996 due to complications of his disease, and it was during a time when he was in a coma for two weeks that the family met his lover named Dan. Dan never left Clyde's room, and it was at that time that the family embraced him for who he was and not for what they thought they wanted him to be.

However, that did not ultimately lead Travis to exposing his secret disdain for Clyde, although he was there for him. Clyde was able to pull through his near-death complications and began to write poetry to help him deal with this fatal disease. He wrote a poem on faith that was published, and he would often share additional poems with family and friends through emails. One Sunday as Travis was preparing to leave for his new life in his new city, he heard an inspirational message on the power of forgiveness and importance of forgiving yourself and asking others whom they may have been holding secretly captive free.

Travis took a long drive and began to cry as he started to think of all the things that Clyde had done for him. Although he wanted Clyde to teach him skills to play sports, talk about girls, and other so-called manly things, he had begun to acknowledge the positive things Clyde had done for him in the past. Which included taking him to the mall, giving him money when he needed it, and verbally giving him positive affirmations when he was down about life. Travis knew it was time for him to come out of his closet of disdain and lightweight hate, it was time for him to come out of the closet of fear and let Clyde know what he had been hiding for so many years because he knew Clyde only had so much time to live and he didn't want him to transition from earth before asking him for forgiveness for what he had been thinking about him for so long.

One evening, days before Travis was to depart for his new city, he went to Clyde's home and acknowledged all that he had felt from his early adolescent years and told him he had been secretly hating and denying him because he was a homosexual. Clyde listened, and after a brief discussion, he forgave Travis for what he had been feeling about him. Clyde used this conversation to have an open discussion about his life and the lifestyle he had chosen, and by the time they were finished with the conversation, they both had a better understanding of each other and decided to dedicate whatever time they had left on earth to be open, honest, and more caring for each other. The burden that was lifted from both brothers was so deep and powerful that they talked more, laughed more, and created a deep bond between them until Clyde passed away in 2005. If Travis had not first acknowledged his wrongs in their relationship, forgave himself, and had the courage to ask Clyde for forgiveness, their relationship may have never been authentic.

Travis moved to his new city and was enjoying his new journey when in 2002, his sisters, Evette and Evonne, wanted him to travel to Chicago, so they could visit some mutual friends. Evonne thought as part of the trip that they could visit their brother Kane, since he was serving his sentence at a prison about an hour outside of Chicago, and besides, they hadn't seen him in over 22 years. Travis had second thoughts about the trip because he was still disappointed that he and Kane never developed a relationship like he thought they should have and was always tired of his mother saying, "Kane always took up with you when you were born, he bought you clothes, and took you everywhere," and Travis would say to himself, all he did was buy me a Tonka truck, move away, get married, have kids, name two of them after me, leave his family, and become an alcoholic and dame dope fiend.... So, Travis's reservations were real. After contemplating whether he wanted to go, being a jetsetter, he decided he would more so because he had never been to Chicago and wanted to see what it was like, and if the visit to see Kane didn't happen, he would not be upset. However, after completing the inmate visitor application and being approved, the thought of seeing Kane after all those years became apparent and Travis needed to be mentally prepared for the encounter.

After spending a few days in Chicago, Travis and his sisters took the trek out to the maximum security prison to see Kane. The odd thing was once they got in the visiting room, they did not immediately recognize Kane and only knew it was him because he looked familiar, and he was the only inmate in the visiting room at the time sitting alone.

The conversation started really casual between Kane and his siblings, however, after small talk about conditions of the facility, Travis asked a bunch of why questions that included, "Why did leave your family? Why did you begin using drugs and alcohol? Why did you break into that famiy's home and try and kill two people?" and to Travis's surprise, Kane, in a calm manner, answered each question with a well thought out response. He did not make any excuses for his behavior and let his siblings know that he was rightfully paying for his mistakes. He said after some long reflection and 14 years behind bars gave him plenty of time to think, he was where he deserved to be, but he was ready to come home but had been discouraged because he had been denied parole on three different occasions. He told them he was sorry for not being there for them while they were growing up and that he was suffering from severe depression and another psychological diagnosis as result of the lifestyle he chose to live. Before they left, Kane asked Travis if he would write him a letter to give to the parole board for his upcoming hearing in a few months. Travis, while he respected Kane's acknowledgement of his wrongs, told him he needed time to reflect on the visit and get back to him once he returned home from the trip. After leaving the facility, for the remainder of the trip to Chicago, all Travis could think about was Kane.

Once Travis came home, he broke down and cried as he entered his house. All the pain that he had felt for not having Kane in his life, and also reflecting on what happened with him and Clyde, gave Travis a new perspective on what his life was to mean moving forward. Travis had spent so much time thinking about what he thought his brothers' role in his life was to be that he never gave it a thought that maybe it was he that was being developed in his childhood to make a difference in his bothers' lives. For far too long, Travis took what society says his roles is to be in the world and follow an order that may have made sense to many others, when in reality, the things that people define as setbacks are only a part of our journey to reach our ultimate destiny. After being in deep thought, Travis realized that although he had some setbacks in his mind because he did not have the type of big brothers he had in mind, that his life was on the path that had already been predestined for the very moment he was in to make a difference in his brothers lives at the appointed time.

Travis wrote a letter to the parole board that was open, honest, and heartfelt. In part, he stated that while he did not have a close relationship with his brother and had not seen him in over 22 years prior to his recent visit, his brothers attitude, forthrightness, and no-excuse posture led him to ask for Kane to be given one opportunity to be paroled, and if he fails while on release, to bring him back to prison to serve his time. While Travis did not know whether he and Kane would ever be as close as they may have been if things were different, he stated they would start a fresh relationship built on mutual trust and understanding and that he forgave Kane for any transgressions he may have committed against him.

Several months later, Kane was granted parole and was released from prison six-months later. Kane moved back to Alabama in 2003 and has since been released from parole. Travis and Kane are not as close as they would have been if they had spent more time together years ago, however, they continued to build upon the foundation of the power of forgiveness that was set that day during the visit to the facility...

You Make the Call

Take a moment and answer the below questions and think about Travis's journey to the road of redemption with his brothers.

1. What do you believe led Travis to asking Clyde for forgiveness?
2. Would Travis been able to forgive Kane if he had not asked Clyde for forgiveness?

Self-Assessment

1. Have you forgiven yourself for your past transgressions?
2. Have you forgiven those who have committed transgressions against you? If not, what steps if any, are you taking to do so?

Affirmation Creed

I am somebody. Although some have labeled me worthless, I know my value.

My current situation will not deter me from living out my purpose.

Too increase my total wellness, I will take advantage of all educational, recreational, and spiritual learning opportunities available to me.

I take full responsibility for my past, present, and future actions.

When I get frustrated, I will seek clarity.

When I am rejected, I will keep a cool head.

When I am depressed, I will stop feeling sorry for myself and get a grip.

When faced with temptation to live my old life, I will exercise my will power.

I will not give up.

I will continue to press forward.

I will act in accordance with my rights, duties, and privileges as a citizen and be a contributing member to my community.

I will make a difference.

Taking Ownership in Your Actions and Decisions

Taking ownership of your actions and decisions is a vital component to having strong character. We need to take ownership of the decisions that we have made and the things that we've done to take account for the damage may have been caused. Stepping up and saying to yourself and others that you were responsible for the good and the bad decisions we have made is a sign of maturity and growth. It is always easy to blame others for what went wrong and take credit for things that resulted in success. It is easy to point fingers and say your life is a result of not having a father or for growing up poor or not becoming a star athlete because your high school coach didn't like you. All these excuses just highlight the need to look deeper into your past and the need to develop mental skills to learn to take ownership of how you make decisions and view life. It doesn't mean that life may have not given you some adversity, what it means is we cannot use our adverse situations as a crutch to not become better people.

The first thing you need to do when you are taking ownership of our bad choices, decisions, and actions is to obligate ourselves to the behavior. Just like a bill that needs to be paid to a utility or mortgage company, you must pay the obligations you make. Obligating, in this context, means taking responsibility and ensuring whatever is due, you take care of it. Obligating yourself to a wrong is the first step in making it right. Acknowledging the obligation will help you with the next important step in taking ownership and that is withdrawing from the behavior.

It is difficult to stop conducting yourself in a manner that is illegal, immoral, and disrespectful if we do not obligate ourselves to those actions. Once you obligate yourself, then we can act towards withdrawing from the behavior. Withdrawing from negative behavior will allow you an opportunity to show growth and development in the areas you need to change. It is easier to obligate yourself to something than to withdraw from the actual behavior, especially if it is something you have done continually over time. The temptation that comes with some of the bad habits and character flaws you have are going to take strong determination and discipline to move on from. That is why accessing your character traits, relationships, forgiveness, and working on your total wellness will put you in a position to conquer the things that has haunted you over time. When you get in a steady pattern of obligating bad behavior and withdrawing from the actions, you can move toward the last component of taking ownership and that is navigating yourself to a different outcome.

Navigating yourself to a different point of view and actions are critical to becoming the best you. Just like a Global Positioning System (GPS), you must put in your hearts and minds a different mapping system, so that you will not continue to recycle your bad behavior and stinking thinking patterns. Navigating your thoughts and placing them into better action plans will show others that we are maturing and growing away from the issues that have brought you down. Embracing the process of obligation, withdrawal, and navigation will help you build your self-worth and value.

This process will not be easy because often people like to do the things that give them instant gratification. Also, the true test will come when you are faced with situations that behaving in certain ways come more natural to you, although you know it is the wrong decision to make. For example, if you have an issue with anger management and you have decided to not let anyone get to you as easily, but it has been a while since anyone has tested you.

The first time someone really gets under your skin and you would normally make a negative comment or even strike the person and you are able to feel the slightest bit of emotion and are able to control yourself, then you know that you have embraced the process. However, if you an emotional response and/or strike the person, you know that you have more work to do in this area. We are all a work in progress, and do not be discouraged because as you continue to use this way of processing your actions, you will grow stronger with time.

....

Case Study: A Second Chance to Make a First Impression

Randy just arrived in Philadelphia as the new Director of Sanitation for the city of Philadelphia, Pennsylvania. He had recently been the sanitation Chief in Portland, Oregon. Randy, an attorney by trade, has been working in the Sanitation business for the last several years. He started out as an associate general counsel for the city of Seattle, Washington. Over the years, Randy had built a solid reputation as a 'clean up man.' He is known for his analytical ability to assess issues, create new processes, and change the culture of a sanitation department. Randy was born and raised on the west coast, and this was his first assignment on the east coast. Randy took on this challenge as a favor, for one of his law school classmates was recently elected mayor of Philadelphia. Randy's wife and children were excited about the move as they enjoyed a few vacations on the east coast throughout the years.

Once Randy got his family settled, he began fiercely looking into the needs of the department, which needed addressed immediately. The department was due for a shake up because of past mismanagement and corruption issues. In lieu of getting to know his leadership team and getting their buy-in to what needed to be done, he started making comments about the department's operations, personnel practices, and demanded immediate change. At home, his wife and children were having a hard time getting adjusted to their home, school, and weather patterns. They moved at the beginning of winter, and it was a major difference from the winters in Portland.

The staff began turning their backs on Randy because they did not understand his management style and he quickly learned 'culture eats strategy for breakfast.' The mayor's office received several complaints from the staff at the department and the mayor called Randy in for a meeting. The mayor told Randy how much confidence he had in him but wanted to discuss the concerns that were raised. Randy confided in the mayor that he has had a difficult time with how they do business in Philadelphia, and that normally, when he arrives to a new department, the staff get right on board. He also let the mayor know his family is having a hard time adjusting to the city and that has played a role in his attitude in the office. Randy let the mayor know that he appreciated him brining him on board to lead the sanitation department and he would make this right.

....

You Make the Call

To earn an opportunity to have a second chance to make a first impression there are authentic actions that need to be exhibited to begin anew. How would you advise Randy in his approach to gain the trust of his team?

A. Call a meeting to apologize to staff and ask for a fresh start.
B. Meet with his direct reports individually
C. Re-roll out his plans after getting to know them better.
D. All the above.
E. None of the above.

....

Self-Assessment

1. What strategies are you using to authentically take ownership of actions and decisions?
2. How will you know when you are showing signs of maturity and not making the same poor decisions?

Affirmation Creed

I am somebody. Although some have labeled me worthless, I know my value.

My current situation will not deter me from living out my purpose.

Too increase my total wellness, I will take advantage of all educational, recreational, and spiritual learning opportunities available to me.

I take full responsibility for my past, present, and future actions.

When I get frustrated, I will seek clarity.

When I am rejected, I will keep a cool head.

When I am depressed, I will stop feeling sorry for myself and get a grip.

When faced with temptation to live my old life, I will exercise my will power.

I will not give up.

I will continue to press forward.

I will act in accordance with my rights, duties, and privileges as a citizen and be a contributing member to my community.

I will make a difference.

Things Take TIME (T.I.M.E.)

One of the first questions people often ask when they find themselves in a difficult season of life is "how long is this going to last?" People who have been convicted of a crime at that moment they are found guilty is how much time are they going to get. For the acronym of time, I want to discuss the strategy you should implement when confronted with issues and concerns. The "T" in time is talent. Each person that is reading this book has talent. While you may feel that whatever you're dealing with is too much to handle, you already have the talent within you to take these issues head on and make a difference in your life. You have the knowledge skills and abilities within you, however, you must channel these talents in a different way in order for your life to mean something more than it has to this point.

The "I" in time is intelligence. Just as much talent you possess, you also have in you an abundance of intelligence. The intelligence you possess will help you utilize your skills to better strategize how you are going to take on the issues you currently face and turn your issues into something that will make your life not only more meaningful but that which will create a positive legacy for those connected to you. You must be smart to cultivate better relationships, use your intelligence to leverage strategies to overcome your obstacles to use your time wisely to produce fruitful endings.

Thirdly, the "M" in time is management. You must learn to manage your talents and intelligence. Managing these two character strengths in the proper format will keep you from some of the poor decisions and stinking thinking patterns that may have been hindering you for some time.

The "E" in time is expectation. You can have all the talent, intelligence, and management skills in the world, but if you do not expect more and better for yourself, all of your hard work will be in vain. Stigmas related to drug and alcohol abuse, incarceration, mental illness, low self-esteem, divorce, and many other issues can cause a person who once had high expectations for themselves to diminish in a split second. Often a person's self-worth and expectations are often tied to what others think and feel about them. You must develop your expectations on your value system and not to people. That is why it is imperative that you expect to be greater than what life is showing you now. No one wants to be on a losing team, everyone wants to be a part of a winner, and even if the team is not winning, if they are playing with a winning mind set and culture, it attracts people to root for them. So, if you are going to make a difference in your life and of those around you, you must have a winner's mindset and expect for your current situation not to define you for the rest of your life.

Case Study: A Story about a Winners Mindset

There was a woman named Faith who was serving a life sentence and had been in prison for nearly 25 years. After the first year in prison, she began working on filing an appeal in the hopes of being released. After her appeal was denied, she became discouraged. She thought she would never have an opportunity to spend time with her sons in the community again as they were two and four years old when she was convicted. Over time, Faith stopped feeling sorry for herself and began working in the prison chapel and volunteering to help out with younger offenders get acclimated to prison life. Although she had no hopes for a new sentence, she began to believe that one day she would be granted clemency or pardoned because a few other inmates had been granted clemency at the end of the last presidential administration.

In preparation for her future release, at least three times per week when someone from her unit was releasing from prison, she would pack out her property to simulate the day she would go home. Many years went by, as well as two more presidential administrations, and she had yet to receive a pardon. This didn't stop her from believing that one day her turn would come; the more others thought she was losing her mind for packing out, the more her confidence grew. She believed that the more she gave to others who had a promise of a release date, that she knew would receive a miracle and be granted a pardon.

She would eventually apply for a pardon a year prior to the end of the most recent presidential administration in hopes that she would be released. She felt something different about this application even though many of her peers and family doubted her. While waiting on the final decision, she kept working with the other inmates, leading bible study and the women's choir, directed plays and skits during the holiday season. After many years of rejection, denials, and years without being there for her children, she was granted a pardon. After her release Faith became a Board Member of a Non-Profit Criminal Justice Reform Organization and dedicated the remainder of her life to public service. Faith winning mindset was at the core of the foundation for her miracle. She took responsibility for her past, developed strategies to use her time in a constructive manner, took ownership of her actions and decisions, and made a difference in the lives of her peers while not knowing if she would ever have her freedom again.

••

You Make the Call

Take a moment to review the below questions regarding Faith's journey.

1. What factors led to Faith believe she would one day be free?

2. How can people maintain a winner's mind set in losing situations?

....

Self-Assessment

1. What principles are you applying to ensure you have an expectation to get through tough seasons in life?

2. How are going to utilize the T.I.M.E. strategy?

Affirmation Creed

I am somebody. Although some have labeled me worthless, I know my value.

My current situation will not deter me from living out my purpose.

Too increase my total wellness, I will take advantage of all educational, recreational, and spiritual learning opportunities available to me.

I take full responsibility for my past, present, and future actions.

When I get frustrated, I will seek clarity.

When I am rejected, I will keep a cool head.

When I am depressed, I will stop feeling sorry for myself and get a grip.

When faced with temptation to live my old life, I will exercise my will power.

I will not give up.

I will continue to press forward.

I will act in accordance with my rights, duties, and privileges as a citizen and be a contributing member to my community.

I will make a difference.

Taking Advantage of all Educational, Recreational and Spiritual Learning Opportunities

It is important to not allow your current situation to deter you from ultimately achieving your goals. Earlier, I discussed the importance of knowing your self-worth and value, the importance of understanding your strengths and areas for improvement, and looking deeply into our relationships that has made a positive and negative impact on your lives. Now that we set the foundation for the book, we must now chart a path to ensure you do not allow the things of the past and your current situation keep you from creating strategies to live out your purpose.

Start by you asking yourself some basic questions: What are my ultimate goals? What will I need to do to put myself in a position to achieve these goals? What short-term goals can I accomplish to meet my long-term goals? These questions are important as you begin to move forward to changing the trajectory of your life. It is imperative that you acknowledge where you are now and where you would like to be in the near and distant future. There will be many obstacles that will try to get you from focusing on what needs to be done to improve your life, so you will need to establish a laser sharp focus. You need to affirm to yourself daily that you will stay the course no matter how difficult the terrain. You are somebody, and you are not only doing this for yourself but for your family and those who are counting you to help make a difference in their lives.

One of the most prominent curriculums taught in undergraduate studies on wellness models is Hettler's wellness model (1984). This model focused on six dimensions of health-related behavior: physical wellness, emotional wellness, spiritual wellness, social wellness, occupational, and intellectual wellness. In order to not allow your current situation to keep you from achieving your goals, you must take advantage of all education, recreational, and spiritual learning opportunities you have access to. Taking care of your total wellness will be imperative for your future success. Let's start first with education. Whatever issues you are dealing with you must deal with the issue by addressing any educational concerns you may have. For instance, if you are incarcerated and you do not have a high school diploma or GED, you must start there. Basic reading, writing, and mathematical skills are a must if you are going to be able to develop the knowledge, skills and abilities to move your life forward. If you do not have the basic skills to be able to articulate your thoughts verbally and in writing, it is going be extremely difficult to start your own business or become gainfully employed.

Reading books, published journals, and other materials will help you develop a stronger vocabulary. This will improve your verbal communication and writing skills, and also give you a broader perspective on life. Studying the issues related to your current situation will also help you improve your life. The more you know, the more you grow.

Physical health and wellness are imperative components to your overall wellness. Developing a workout plan on your level can help reduce stress, excess weight, and improve your outlook on life. This will help you develop discipline and focus which can also be used in other areas you have identified to improve your life. Physical wellness is just one component of overall wellness. You must work on your mental wellness. Making healthy choices will help your attitude. Working out and eating right are just two components to total wellness. Taking time to address any mental issues that you may be dealing with as a result of your current situation is imperative to your total wellness. Do not be ashamed to see a licensed professional counselor, psychologist, or psychiatrist to address the concerns you have about your current or past issues. This is a sign of maturity and that says you are ready to face these issues head on and will help you move forward.

Another key component to total wellness is feeding your spirit. Educating your mind and working out, making healthy choices, and seeking mental health are keys to a healthy lifestyle; however, without something feeding your spirit on a continual basis, none of the above subjects will have a lasting impact on your life. Whatever your religious beliefs may be, if you are not connected to a spiritual leader and environment that is built on faith, hope, and overcoming issues and forgiving yourself and others, none of the plans you set in motion to change your life will work. Life is hard, it is difficult, it is full of many ups and downs. However, the life you live can be filled with a type of peace and joy that surpasses all understanding.

Connecting your life to a purpose greater than your own will help you set your life on a path that will help you not only deal with your current and past issues, it will put in a posture to be able to deal with all of your future issues and assist you to significantly reduce you from making the same life altering choices over and over and over again. You cannot take this journey alone, and if you think you can or you feel you know it all, you are sadly mistaken.

A very influential religious leader once said something very profound, he stated that if you are the smartest person in your circle, you need some new friends because you should always have people pulling you up and you should always be in a position help pull others up. You need people to challenge yourself by making associations with people wiser than you, so that you can be in a position to improve your life on a consistent basis.

....

Case Study: When Early Success Cause Distractions

After graduating with honors from college, Alana had visions of completing her Master of Business Administration degree and eventually becoming a Chief Executive Officer of a marketing firm. She planned to work two to three years at a Fortune 500 company, then go to graduate school part-time. Within the first year of her working at her firm, the company's vice president took a liking to her and she began being promoted and receiving large bonuses each year. While Alana received instant success, she did not keep with the industry trends and new strategies to maintain her competitive edge. Alana did not make any friends at the firm because some of her colleagues were jealous of her success, and they felt she didn't have to work as hard as them because the "boss" liked her.

On a personal level, success had made Alana lazy and was losing focus on her family and friends and had stopped living an active lifestyle because, in the back of her mind, she had it all. Alana enjoyed bike riding and taking hikes in the mountains to stay in shape. Alana's company merged with a larger firm and her vice president was not retained. Due to Alana's lack of performance, she soon learned she was not going to be retained. She received a large severance package and decided to sell her stock options. While battling depression due to being out of employment, Alana began to re-focus on the things that mattered to her the most: her family and close friends.

While weighing her options for the future, she thought about her dreams of owning her own marketing firm. However, she knew she needed to get additional training on the latest industry standards. She recalled wanting to have a Master of Business Administration (MBA) degree, but her initial success delayed that goal. Alana started working out again and it made her feel a sense of joy she had not felt in a long time. She wants to develop strategies that will have a positive, lasting impact on her life.

You Make the Call

Early success can lull anyone onto a self-conscious sleep and distract you from focusing and staying sharp. How would advise Alana to develop a plan of action to create new strategies to get her career back on track.

1. Go back to school and get her MBA.
2. Start a small marketing firm with the stock option money she received.
3. Give up her dream and start a new career.
4. Another option.

Self-Assessment

1. What are the tools you are working on to ensure you can achieve your goals for your present and future?
2. What effective strategies can be applied to staying focused and determined?

Affirmation Creed

I am somebody. Although some have labeled me worthless, I know my value.

My current situation will not deter me from living out my purpose.

Too increase my total wellness, I will take advantage of all educational, recreational, and spiritual learning opportunities available to me.

I take full responsibility for my past, present, and future actions.

When I get frustrated, I will seek clarity.

When I am rejected, I will keep a cool head.

When I am depressed, I will stop feeling sorry for myself and get a grip.

When faced with temptation to live my old life, I will exercise my will power.

I will not give up.

I will continue to press forward.

I will act in accordance with my rights, duties, and privileges as a citizen and be a contributing member to my community.

I will make a difference.

Developing a Personal Development Plan

The Quality Assurance Agency (QAA) in the United Kingdom defines a personal development plan (PDP) in part as articulating personal goals and evaluating progress towards achievement and encourages a positive attitude to learning throughout life. Understanding the significance of strategic planning and creating a vision for your life will be vital to you becoming a better you and making a difference. Developing a strategy begins with understanding your value, working on your strengths and areas for improvement. You must begin to forgive yourself and others. Taking responsibility for your past, present and future, and working on your total wellness is also a key component to a solid PDP. Once you have taken an inventory of these things, you can set out on a path to put your life on a trail that will lead to not only a life of significance but of peace and joy. Looking into each of these areas and developing a long-term strategy with easily attainable short-term goals will be a major part of your success. You cannot wait until things get better to begin to move your life forward. You cannot make any changes in your life until you take the first step forward. Knowing where you have been and acknowledging where you are will be the foundation of looking ahead and charting a new path.

A recent review of the PDP literature (Gough, 2003) suggests that when expressed as a set of actions and processes, PDP contains elements of planning, doing, recording, reviewing, and evaluating. You must begin to visualize in your mind where you want to be in the next 5, 10, 20 years and beyond. As you see where you want to be, visualize what it will take to get there. If it is a college degree you wish to obtain, visualize hearing your name being called as you walk across the stage. Once you see the goal, now you must chart out the path that it will take to attain the degree step by step, and as you follow each step, get to the next and will be closer to finishing. You must see the goal, say it to yourself, and then seize it by following the process to ultimately achieving it. This can be done by following the keys (K.E.Y.S) to success.

The K.E.Y.S.
(Knowledge-Exercise-Yearning-Simplicity) to Success

There are many paths that people take to achieving their aspirations in life. There is not just one way to obtain success. However, there are a few simple principles that can be followed to do so. First, gaining as much knowledge on the subject is the first step. Studying and researching the topic will be vital. Gathering insight will help propel you through each stage in the process. You cannot go into anything blind about the subject and believe that you are going to finish what you started. This is where taking advantage of all educational, recreational, and spiritual learning opportunities become more prevalent.

The second principle to the keys of success is exercise. By exercising your knowledge through reading, experiencing the process first hand, and adding repetition to the process your knowledge of the subject will grow and your capacity to expand will be created. Exercising your knowledge base will help develop discipline to properly handle distractions that may cross your path during the transition.

The third principle to the keys of success is yearning. While knowledge and exercise of the goal will help develop discipline, you may become broad with the process if the goal you are trying to obtain takes a long time. You must continue to yearn for more, yearn to have the most knowledge about your goals, and to exercise what you know to be able to expand your capacity. Celebrate the small victories along the way but do not become complacent. The yearning and desire to grow will help feed your hunger to finish what you started.

The fourth principle to the keys to success is simplicity. Keeping your strategies and objectives in the proper perspective will help you develop the other three principles of knowledge, exercise, and yearning. Simplicity will assist you with obtaining goals within the larger goals you set and make things less complicated for you to make sure you are on the path to achievement. Stick to a simple schedule that works for you, remember, life is a marathon, not a sprint. Celebrate the small victories along the way, but do not become complacent. Work at your own pace, and if you have someone in your life that is working on the same goal, do not compete with them. They may finish first, but remember, as long as you finish, that is all that matters.

....

Case Study: Preparing for a Marathon

Carlos was excited about preparing for his first marathon. He began running five years ago because he wanted to change his appearance and get in shape. He was entering his late 30's when he started running and was

41

considered obese according to the Body Mass Index (BMI) scale. Carlos began recording what he ate every day to evaluate his food intake. He started assessing his fitness level and set small goals, such as running five minutes without stopping, then 10, then 20 until he felt comfortable with recording one mile at a time. Once he could jog 30 minutes without stopping, he decided within a year he would participate in a 5k (3.1 miles) race, and in two years, he hoped to participate in a ten mile race, and in three years, he would participate in a half marathon. Carlos was able to meet his fitness goals, change his diet, and the only meat he consumed was fish. By year three, Carlos ran his first half marathon in just over two hours.

A few weeks after competing in his first half marathon, Carlos moved to another city. Due to the transition, his fitness levels dropped and his eating habits changed when he lived in a hotel for two months. Although he continued running, he was a few steps slower. After several months of trying to get back in shape, Carlos is seeing minimal results and he is scheduled to run his first marathon in ten months.

Carlos is contemplating whether he will be able to be prepared for the marathon in ten months. He is unsure of himself and doesn't want to feel pressured to compete in the race, but Carlos has always been a person to try and stick to the timelines he has set for himself.

. . . .

You Make the Call

Participating in a marathon takes time, focus, preparation, training and repetition. Please answer the below questions and advise Carlos.

1. What strategic plans should Carlos implement to prepare for the marathon? What advice is your group going to give him and why?
2. Should he wait another two to three years to run the marathon since it took him three years to run his first half marathon?

. . . .

Self-Assessment

1. What are the key components to achieving the goals you have set?
2. What are the factors to following each step of the process?

Affirmation Creed

I am somebody. Although some have labeled me worthless, I know my value.

My current situation will not deter me from living out my purpose.

Too increase my total wellness, I will take advantage of all educational, recreational, and spiritual learning opportunities available to me.

I take full responsibility for my past, present, and future actions.

When I get frustrated, I will seek clarity.

When I am rejected, I will keep a cool head.

When I am depressed, I will stop feeling sorry for myself and get a grip.

When faced with temptation to live my old life, I will exercise my will power.

I will not give up.

I will continue to press forward.

I will act in accordance with my rights, duties, and privileges as a citizen and be a contributing member to my community.

I will make a difference.

Making a Difference

For many, if not most, the meaning of citizenship is a topic left un-reflected in daily life (Conyer, Crew, and Searing, 1991). Taking the necessary steps to acting in accordance with your rights, duties, and privileges and become a better citizen and a contributing member of your community is important and will have a lasting impact on your life. There are many areas in life for us to act as a good citizen and person who positively contributes to their communities. They include taking an active role in your heritage, the democratic process, special groups that may be active in your area, local, state, and federal government, and your community and family.

Being a good citizen is a reflection of what you take pride in, and the first should be your family. Taking care of your home, cutting the grass, and cleaning the areas you are responsible for is important. Having a driver's license, car insurance, a copy of your birth certificate and social security card, health insurance for you and your family, and knowing your credit score are also key components of good citizenship.

Knowing your family history and where you originate will help you take pride in who you are and the traditions that come from the place you family came from. This will make for interesting conversations with your family and friends as you navigate through history of cultural norms and traditions.

Being an active member in the democratic process is a key component to good citizenship. This includes voting, encouraging others to vote, attending public meetings, and giving feedback to public officials. Knowing who your mayor, city council persons, governor, chief of police, sheriff, county leaders are important. This will keep you current on the issues that are in the forefront of your neighborhood, city, state, and the country.

If you currently do not have voting rights, find out what steps it will take to get them back in good standing. Each state has its own voting laws, and it is imperative for you to know what your state requires.

Special groups, such as the chamber of commerce, volunteer organizations, and churches are great to be involved in. Attending a local church will help you grow spiritually and should be the foundation of your total wellness. If you are planning to open a business, becoming a member of the chamber of commerce will help develop good networking opportunities and a place to market your business. Volunteering in your community will make a difference in many ways. It may be personally fulfilling to know that you gave of yourself to help others, and it is a great way to give back to your community.

Duke University completed a study in 2009 on "Peace of Mind" and found eight factors that contribute to emotional and mental stability are: 1) The absence of suspicion and resentment, 2) Not living in the past, 3) Not wasting time and energy on fighting conditions you cannot change, 4) Force yourself to stay involved in the living world, 5) Refuse to indulge in self-pity when life deals you a raw deal, 6) Cultivate the old fashioned virtues: love, humor, compassion, and loyalty, 7) Do not expect too much of yourself, and 8) Find something bigger than yourself to believe in.

Who you are? At this point of the book, you should be more aware of your strengths, areas needed for improvement. You should have taken a closer view into the positive and negative relationships that have shaped your life, and began to understand the power of forgiveness of yourself and others. Thus you should begin to start developing a strategic plan and vision to move your life forward in a direction which will lead you to live in your purpose. Making a difference will not be easy, but it will be worth the journey you will take when you begin to change the way you think, communicate, and act.

Personal integrity should be at the foundation of your mission to making a difference. You often hear that integrity is doing the right thing when no one is watching and this is true. However, the definition is not that simple. Integrity is doing the right thing, even if it costs you something. When you are faced with a decision that can be right by law or from a value system, it does not mean that decision is always correct. For example, you may be confronted with deciding to do something that you are uncomfortable with and the choice you decide to make may have severe consequences, even though it is the right decision. Making the right choice may cost you relationships; it may cause you more time to get to your goals, however, it is a sign of growth and maturity. Making a difference is about the lasting impact. Playing the long game may not feel good in the short term, but you will be able to live with yourself, and ultimately, things will fall into place.

Sacrifice is also a major component to making a difference. To alter and modify your current situation, you will need to sacrifice some old habits and thought patterns and create new ones. You may have to sacrifice some relationships and hobbies. Taking a holistic approach to creating a new life will take the type of discipline where sacrifice is leading the charge. Having the courage to face your fears will be pivotal to your success. You have to develop a face everything and rise mentality and not a fake everything and run attitude. The process is going to be challenging, and at times, to tough endure. However, following the core objectives outlined in this book will provide you the tools to set your life on a path of change and significance. Remember, you are somebody, and others are counting you to make a difference to create a legacy that will make a shift in the culture for generations to come.

....

Self-Assessment
1. How will you apply the principles outlined in this book to prepare yourself for your future?
2. How are you going to make a difference in your community and live out your purpose?

Affirmation Creed

I am somebody. Although some have labeled me worthless, I know my value.

My current situation will not deter me from living out my purpose.

Too increase my total wellness, I will take advantage of all educational, recreational, and spiritual learning opportunities available to me.

I take full responsibility for my past, present, and future actions.

When I get frustrated, I will seek clarity.

When I am rejected, I will keep a cool head.

When I am depressed, I will stop feeling sorry for myself and get a grip.

When faced with temptation to live my old life, I will exercise my will power.

I will not give up.

I will continue to press forward.

I will act in accordance with my rights, duties, and privileges as a citizen and be a contributing member to my community.

I will make a difference.

References

Baumeister, R.F., Leary, M. (1995). The need to belong: Desire for interpersonal attachments as a fundamental human motivation. Psychological Bulletin, 117, 497-52.

Carroll, P.J., Arkin, R.M., Shade, C.K. (2011). Possible selves & Self-Doubt: A poverty of desired possibility. Social Psychological & Personality Science 2(2). 190-198. SAGE Publications.

Critical Thinking as Defined by the National Council for Excellence in Critical Thinking, 1987. A statement by Michael Scriven & Richard Paul, presented at the 8th Annual International Conference on Critical Thinking and Education Reform, Summer 1987. http://www.criticalthinking.org/pages/defining-critical-thinking/766

Duke University (2009). Study on "Peace of Mind." Retrieved from: https://bible.org/illustration/duke-university-study

Dunn, H.L. (1961). High level wellness. Arlington, VA: Beatty.

Facione, P.A. (1990). Critical Thinking. A statement of expert consensus for purposes of educational assessment and instruction. Milbrae, CA. The California Free Press.

Gough, D.A. (2003). A Systematic Map & Synthesis Review of Effectiveness of Personal Development Planning for Improvement of Student Learning. London: EPPI-Central Social Sciences Research Unit.

Hettler, W. (1984). Wellness: Encouraging a life pursuit of excellence. Health Values. Achieving high level wellness, 8, 13-17.

Jones, E.E., Berglas, S. (1978). Control of Attributions about the self through handicapping strategies. The appeal of alcohol and the role of underachievement. Personality and Social Psychology Bulletin, 4, 200-206.

Kamen, Randy, Dr. (2012). Article: The Power of Forgiveness. Retrieved from: http://www.huffingtonpost.com/randy-kamen-gredinger-edd/forgiveness_b_2006882.html

Kennedy, M. Fisher, M.B, & Ennis, R. H. (1991). Critical thinking literature review and the need for research. In L. Idol & B.F. Jones (Eds.). Educational values and cognitive instructions: Implications for Reform (p 11-40). Hillsdale, New Jersey: Lawrence Erblaem and Associates.

Maslow, A. H. (1970). Motivation and Personality. New York: Harper & Row.

Paul, R.W. (1992). Critical thinking: What, Why, and How? New Directions for Community Colleges, 1992. (77), 3-24.

Steger, M.F., Frazier, P., Oishi, S., & Kaler (2006). The Meaning in life questionnaire: Assessing Presence & Search for Meaning in Life. Journal of Counseling Psychology, 53, 80-93.

Van Tongeren, D.R., Green, J.D., Nook, J.N., Davis, D.E., Ramos, M. (2015). Forgiveness Increases Meaning in Life. Social Psychology and Personality Science. Vol 6(1), 47-55. SAGE Publications.

Van Tongeren, D.R., Welch, R.D, Davis, D.E., Green, J.D., & Worthington, E.L. Jr. (2012). Priming

Virtue: Forgiveness & Justice elicit divergent moral judgments among religious individuals. Journal of Positive Psychology, 7, 405-415.

Willingham, D.T. (2007). Critical Thinking: Why is it so hard to teach? American Educator, 8.